The Future of
TECHNOLOGY

What Is the Future of
Artificial
Intelligence?

John Allen

ReferencePoint
Press®

San Diego, CA

© 2017 ReferencePoint Press, Inc.
Printed in the United States

For more information, contact:
ReferencePoint Press, Inc.
PO Box 27779
San Diego, CA 92198
www.ReferencePointPress.com

LIBRARY OF CONGRESS CATALOGING-IN-PUBLICATION DATA

Names: Allen, John, 1957- author.
Title: What is the future of artificial intelligence? / John Allen.
Description: San Diego, CA : ReferencePoint Press, Inc., 2017. | Series: The future of technology | Audience: Grades 9 to 12. | Includes bibliographical references and index.
Identifiers: LCCN 2016011959 (print) | LCCN 2016012999 (ebook) | ISBN 9781682820605 (hardback) | ISBN 9781682820612 (eBook)
Subjects: LCSH: Artificial intelligence--Juvenile literature. | Technological innovations--Juvenile literature. | Machine learning--Juvenile literature.
Classification: LCC Q335.4 .A45 2017 (print) | LCC Q335.4 (ebook) | DDC 006.3--dc23
LC record available at http://lccn.loc.gov/2016011959

Contents

Important Events in the Development of Artificial Intelligence

1950
British mathematician Alan Turing publishes "Computing Machinery and Intelligence," a groundbreaking paper on artificial intelligence (AI).

1990
Rodney Brooks's paper "Elephants Don't Play Chess" revives the field of neural networks.

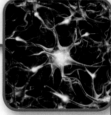

1957
Al Newell and Herbert Simon create the General Problem Solver, a device for solving complex math problems.

1968
Stanley Kubrick's film *2001: A Space Odyssey* brings the idea of a machine with human-level intelligence to a wide audience.

| 1950 | 1960 | 1970 | 1980 | 1990 |

1956
John McCarthy coins the term *artificial intelligence* at the Dartmouth College conference on AI.

1970
Computer scientist Gordon Moore predicts that computing power will double about every two years.

1979
Stanford University scientists demonstrate MYCIN, an expert computer system for treating blood infections.

1962
Unimation, the first industrial robot company, is founded.

1973
The Lighthill Report for the British government kills funding for AI research by claiming that machines can never perform simple acts of intelligence.

1996
A computer at Argonne National Laboratory produces a major mathematical proof that shows signs of creativity.

2006
An Israeli company introduces Waze, an AI-based satellite navigation app for drivers.

2002
The company iRobot creates an autonomous robot vacuum cleaner called Roomba.

2008
Apple releases a smartphone with a speech recognition app by Google that is 92 percent accurate.

| 1995 | 2000 | 2005 | 2010 | 2015 |

2005
Stanley, a Google-designed robot software system, wins the Defense Advanced Research Projects Agency Grand Challenge for self-driving vehicles.

2011
IBM's AI software platform Watson defeats former champion human competitors on the quiz show *Jeopardy!*

1997
Deep Blue, an IBM supercomputer, defeats world champion Garry Kasparov in a chess match.

2016
Google's AI computer system wins a match over the South Korean champion at Go, a complex and ancient board game.

Introduction

Fast Track for a Supercomputer

From Theory to Application

Artificial intelligence (AI) is a branch of computer science that aims to create machines able to perform tasks that normally require human intelligence. Computers are designed to accomplish these tasks through activities such as speech recognition, problem solving, learning, and planning. An important part of artificial intelligence is knowledge engineering, by which machines gather and employ huge amounts of data related to the world. Another is machine learning, or the ability of a computer to use data to perform a task with increased accuracy or efficiency. Machine learning makes use of algorithms, which are mathematical operations for solving problems. Artificial intelligence is also closely related to the field of robotics. Robots employ artificial intelligence to manipulate objects and navigate in the real world. There are two main approaches to AI. One tries to make machines simulate human reasoning to solve problems, and the other focuses on the unique properties of computer systems to perform tasks successfully.

Making it big in New York City often means hiring a large staff and moving into a hip new building downtown. In 2014 IBM's Watson made just such a high-profile move. Watson is a natural language cognitive computing service—a fancy term for a computer with artificial intelligence. Watson enables a company to interact with its own data source and ask questions about it in ordinary language. IBM's prize computer system has already proved itself in a very public venue: a television quiz show. In 2011 Watson squared off on *Jeopardy!* against two of the show's greatest former champions. After three days of play, Watson had brushed aside its human competitors and earned a $1 million prize. The supercomputer—which received the questions instantly as text and so did not have to "listen" to them—was able to sort through its 200 million pages of possible answers and trigger the buzzer with astonishing speed. It is this ability to rapidly process a mountain of data that makes Watson such an exciting new business tool. "Watson is about Big Data," says financial reporter Bob Pisani. "It is about ingesting vast amounts of information on specific subjects—medicine, law, travel, retail, metallurgy, oil and gas, whatever—and allowing a user to query the data to look for patterns, assist in a diagnosis, assist in a legal argument, make a decision on where to drill for oil, almost anything."[1]

WORDS IN CONTEXT

algorithm
A step-by-step procedure for solving a problem.

Computer systems like IBM's Watson that employ artificial intelligence already affect people's lives daily, and this influence continues to grow. Artificial intelligence includes a car's dashboard computer, which can instantly display a map and provide verbal directions so a driver can avoid snarled traffic and reach his or her destination more quickly. AI programs gather data about a person's search history on a computer, using it to tailor ads to the person's specific interests. AI also can help a doctor diagnose a patient's condition more accurately by drawing on vast data banks of medical histories. Homes equipped with AI technology can adjust the temperature and humidity, turn lights off and on automatically, and call the police in case of an emergency. "We live in an era of intelligent technology," says science writer Jurica Dujmovic. "Our watches tell us not only the time, but they also remind us to exercise. Our phones recommend the best places to dine, and our computers predict our preferences, helping us to do our daily work more efficiently."[2]

Watson, a computer developed by IBM, competed against two human opponents on the television game show Jeopardy! in 2011. Equipped with artificial intelligence, the computer handily defeated Ken Jennings (left) and Brad Rutter (right), two of the show's greatest former champions.

Risks and Hopes for the Future

In contrast to this positive outlook, pop culture has often depicted AI in a darker light. Novels such as Isaac Asimov's *I, Robot* and films such as *2001: A Space Odyssey*, *Blade Runner*, *The Matrix*, and *Avengers: Age of Ultron* show the dangerous consequences when thinking machines gain too much power over humans. Some scientists believe the premise of these stories is not so far-fetched. They worry about where AI is heading—especially the growing reliance on machines to oversee human activities. They point to incidents like the 2010 Flash Crash, when complex computer trading programs on Wall Street caused a sudden meltdown in stock prices. Experts warn that without human controls, computer systems could someday malfunction and wreck the economy, damage the environment, or start a nuclear war—much like the villainous supercomputers in science fiction movies.

For now, however, such nightmare scenarios remain the stuff of fiction. Artificial intelligence today is at a very early stage of development, with computer systems only beginning to exhibit abilities such as learning, adapting to new circumstances, communicating in English (or some other language), and manipulating objects with robotics. Scientists foresee a time when AI will not only coordinate large systems such as air travel and energy production, but will also help humans be more creative in their everyday lives. And one day, as computing power continues to increase exponentially, a machine may actually become self-aware, able to think about itself and its role in the world. Or humans may join with machines to form cyborgs—part human, part robot—with longer life spans and still-undreamt-of capabilities. "Everything we have of value as human beings, as a civilization, is the result of our intelligence," says Stuart Russell, a computer scientist at the University of California–Berkeley, "and what AI could do is essentially be a power tool that magnifies human intelligence and gives us the ability to move our civilization forward in all kinds of ways."[3] Whatever happens, the future for artificial intelligence promises to be stranger and more surprising than anything today's technology experts can imagine.

Chapter 1

Making Machines That Can Think

A child learns to write by looking at letters, seeing how they are formed, and then reproducing them on paper. The child generally needs to see a symbol or picture only once in order to recognize it, even if it is viewed from different angles. By contrast, machines have always required hundreds and even thousands of attempts to identify symbols or pictures. In December 2015, however, a trio of researchers introduced a software program that enables a computer to learn visually from as little data as a human requires. The program runs on an algorithm that memorizes general shapes. The computer is then able to draw the shapes in rough copies using a stylus controlled by a robotic arm. In a demonstration, the symbols drawn by the computer—which included odd squiggles and letters from Sanskrit, a language from India—looked very similar to the models and almost the same as the versions done by a child. "For the first time, we think we have a machine system that can learn a large class of visual concepts in ways that are hard to distinguish from human learners,"[4] says Joshua Tenenbaum, a scientist at the Massachusetts Institute of Technology (MIT) and cocreator of the new software program. The researchers also asked the machine and a set of human volunteers to invent new characters in the same style as those they had been shown. The machine's invented symbols looked the same as the ones created by the volunteers.

The Turing Test and the Dartmouth Conference

Tenenbaum and his research partners are determined to reduce the gap between human learning and machine learning, a gap

During World War II, British mathematician and computer scientist Alan Turing invented this machine, a primitive computer, to break Nazi codes. Turing later became known for the eponymous Turing test, a way to test a computer's ability to exhibit intelligence that is indistinguishable from that of a human.

that they insist is still vast. Their project, like hundreds more in research labs around the world, is continuing a decades-long quest to create artificial intelligence. Basically, AI is a scientific field devoted to understanding thought processes and behavior, with the goal of building computer systems that can think and learn from their environment.

AI research goes back to World War II, when scientists began to use computers to solve nonnumerical problems. One of its first great theorists was the British mathematician and computer scientist Alan Turing. During the war, Turing devised a machine to break the Nazis' codes. In 1950 he published a groundbreaking paper on AI called "Computing Machinery and Intelligence." The paper opened with Turing's famous announcement, "I propose to consider the question, 'Can machines think?'"[5] His conclusion was a sort of qualified yes. He believed that machines could be made to mimic human thought processes so well that they would be accepted as being able to think. Turing became known for his Turing test, which he also called the imitation game. This was a way to test a machine's ability to exhibit intelligence that is indistinguishable from that of a human.

In 1956 interest in thinking machines led a group of scientists to meet at Dartmouth College in Hanover, New Hampshire. The goal of the Dartmouth conference was to discuss how to define intelligence and whether a computer system could simulate it. Although the gathering made little progress, several research topics that were suggested there are still relevant to AI research. These include neural networks (computer networks based on the arrangement of the central nervous system in animals), programming a computer to use a language, and self-improvement for machines. The most notable event at the conference occurred when Dartmouth professor John McCarthy coined the term *artificial intelligence*. (Scientists being scientists, the term was immediately criticized for being imprecise.)

The Dartmouth gathering might have been more successful had the group paid more attention to a pair of attendees who were invited almost as an afterthought. Al Newell and Herbert Simon, two young researchers from Carnegie Mellon University, had already invented their own thinking machine—dubbed the Logical Theorist—earlier that year. Simon had compiled heuristics, or practical rules of thumb, that people use to solve geometry problems and that could be programmed into a computer. Newell had introduced a programming language that could imitate the processes of human memory. The following year Newell and Simon created a device they called the General Problem Solver, which they believed could solve the most complex mathematical problems, given the proper description. Although the new machine proved a disappointment overall, the duo's approach to programming a computer to solve problems was extremely influential. Newell and Simon went on to found their own artificial intelligence laboratory at Carnegie Mellon.

The Imitation Game

In a 1951 paper, British mathematician Alan Turing proposed an exercise to decide if a machine displays intelligence. The test involves the following scenario. There are three rooms, each connected to the others via the screen and keyboard of a teletype. In one room is a man or woman, in another room a computer, and in the third an interrogator. The interrogator asks questions and receives answers to determine which of the contestants is the machine. Turing claimed that within fifty years it would be possible to program computers so that the average interrogator would not have more than a 70 percent chance of making the right choice after five minutes of questioning.

The imitation game, or Turing test, has fascinated AI researchers for decades. Through the years many programs were developed in an attempt to pass the Turing test, but none succeeded. In 2014 news stories announced that a computer program named Eugene Goostman at the University of Reading in Great Britain had passed the test. But Eugene proved to be a so-called chatbot programmed with a rote script, not a computer carrying on an intelligent conversation.

Ultimately, Turing's point was that people would come to think of machines as being intelligent. "I believe that at the end of the century," he wrote, "the use of words and general educated opinion will have altered so much that one will be able to speak of machines thinking without expecting to be contradicted." In this Turing proved to be correct.

A.M. Turing, "Computing Machinery and Intelligence," *Mind*, 1950. www.loebner.net.

Optimism and Disappointment

Newell and Simon saw that the first step to creating artificial intelligence was making a machine that could not only solve equations but also figure out how to solve equations. Soon other researchers followed their lead. They began to focus on symbolic reasoning, which is the way the human mind uses symbols and rules to approach a problem-solving task. The goal of their research was to simulate how humans think, and not simply to solve problems correctly regardless of the method.

This period from the late 1950s through the mid-1970s was one of great optimism about the possibilities for AI. "There are now in the world machines that think, that learn and create," Newell claimed in 1958. "Moreover, their ability to do these things is going to increase rapidly until—in a visible future—the range of problems they can handle will be coextensive [roughly equal] with the range to which the human mind has been applied."[6]

Newell and Simon predicted that within a decade, digital computers would discover new mathematical theorems and write symphonic music. In 1970 cognitive scientist Marvin Minsky announced that a machine with the intelligence of an average human being was only a few years away. This kind of enthusiasm helped attract millions in funding for AI research.

However, most of the euphoric claims about AI proved to be premature. Researchers failed to make good on their early predictions of what computers would be able to accomplish. At the same time, critics arose to challenge the whole premise of artificial intelligence. They argued that machines are not able to think and make decisions in the same sense as humans do. Instead, they believed computers are capable only of stringing together calculations to solve trivial problems.

A devastating example of this critique was the so-called Lighthill Report. In 1973 James Lighthill, a professor of mathematics at Cambridge University, wrote an analysis of AI research for the British government. In the report, Lighthill claimed that scientists in the field had failed to account for combinatorial explosion, the idea that a simple calculation that works with two or three variables becomes hopelessly complicated as the number of variables is increased, as in messy real-world problems. "In no part of the field have discoveries made so far produced the major impact that was promised,"[7] Lighthill observed. The Lighthill Report convinced the British government to withdraw funding for AI research, and other governments followed suit, including that of the United States.

Many scientists agreed with Lighthill that machines would likely never be able to store and employ the vast amount of data required to perform simple acts of intelligence, such as recognizing objects or using commonsense reasoning. McCarthy, outraged by the report, flew to the United Kingdom to debate Lighthill on live television about AI's true potential. However, the damage was done. The result was two periods—the first from 1974 to 1980 and the second from 1987 to 1993—in which money for research dried up and numerous scientists abandoned the field. These so-called AI winters threatened to end the quest for machines that could think.

In hindsight it is easy to see that a key problem with AI research at the time was the severe limitation scientists faced in computing power. "Early [computer] programs were necessarily limited in scope by the size and speed of memory and processors and by the relative clumsiness of the early operating systems and languages,"[8] observes Bruce G. Buchanan, a mathematician and former president of the Association for the Advancement of

AI Is Unstoppable at Go

A computer's recent victory in an ancient board game made Deep Blue's win against chess world champion Garry Kasparov seem like child's play. In March 2016 an AI program built by Google's DeepMind lab defeated the South Korean world champion of Go, a game that originated in ancient China. Only a year before, experts had declared that a computer had no chance of defeating a human competitor in the game. The reason is that Go is orders of magnitude more complex than chess. In Go, players move stones on a square board marked off in a nineteen-by-nineteen-line grid. Whereas a chess player has twenty possible first moves, a Go player must choose among 361 possible openings. Over the course of a game, there are more possible positions than atoms in the universe. The game has been a focal point of AI research because winning at it requires pattern-recognition skills and intuition normally reserved for the cleverest human players.

AlphaGo, the Google Go-playing program, owes its success to advances in neural networks and deep learning. AlphaGo trained for its match by ingesting 30 million sample Go moves by the top human players. Then it played thousands of Go games against itself to learn how to evaluate board positions and make estimates on the effectiveness of each move. AlphaGo's opponent, Lee Se-dol, admitted, "All the traditional or classical beliefs we have had about Go so far, I have come to question them a little bit based on my experience with AlphaGo."

Quoted in Elise Hu, "Achievement Unlocked: Google AlphaGo A.I. Wins Go Series, 4-1," NPR, March 17, 2016. www.npr.org.

Artificial Intelligence. For computers even to approach the break-throughs of AI, they had to undergo a significant upgrade.

Deep Blue and a Revival of Interest

As it happened, such an upgrade was just getting under way, leading to the exponential growth of processing power for computers. This development confirmed Moore's law, a prediction made in 1970 by computer scientist Gordon Moore. Moore foresaw that the overall processing power for computers—made possible by squeezing more transistors onto a silicon microchip—would double about every two years. Relentless improvement of these microprocessors led to the explosion in digital technology that continues to shape the modern world.

After years of hype and empty promises, AI research gained new momentum and began to show real progress. One notable breakthrough came in 1996, when a computer program produced a major mathematical proof. The program, written by researchers at Argonne National Laboratory in Lemont, Illinois, proved that a set of three equations is equivalent to Boolean algebra, the group of rules that governs relationships among sets. In doing so, the Argonne computer solved a problem that had stumped the world's top mathematicians for sixty years. The proof showed unmistakable signs of creativity, as when a human mind receives a flash of insight. "It's a sign of power, of reasoning power," said Larry Wos, supervisor of the Argonne project. "We've taken a quantum leap forward."[9]

In May 1997 public awareness of AI's potential received a boost from a celebrated chess match. An IBM supercomputer dubbed Deep Blue defeated the world champion grandmaster Garry Kasparov in a closely contested series of games. Some news stories hailed Deep Blue's triumph as a historic break-through for computer science, while others saw it as a humiliating sign that the human brain was inferior to a machine. Ironically, Deep Blue's success was aided by a human flaw. One of the computer's early moves—a mistake based on a programming glitch, as it turned out—appeared so sophisticated that Kasparov suspected his mechanical opponent of hatching some complex

Viewers watch the now-famous series of chess games between Russian champion Garry Kasparov and IBM's computer Deep Blue. The computer's victory prompted some people to proclaim the event a historic breakthrough in computer science and others to view it as a humiliating defeat of human intelligence against machine intelligence.

strategy he could not fathom. Unnerved, the Russian champion outthought himself throughout the match. Deep Blue never got weary or flustered.

Two months later, on July 4, AI was again in the news. The National Aeronautics and Space Administration (NASA) Pathfinder mission landed an autonomous robotics system on the surface of Mars. The landing module and its rover on wheels, named *Sojourner*, used AI principles to gather and send 2.3 billion bits of information back to Earth. These included 16,500 images from the landing module, 550 images from the rover, more than 15 chemical analyses of rocks and soil, and detailed data on winds and weather conditions. Pathfinder demonstrated that smart machines could replace astronauts and extend humanity's reach into outer space.

Approaches to AI

Examples of success in AI-related projects resulted in waves of new funding and an excitement about the possibilities for AI that continues to this day. AI research branched off into several subfields, some of which reached back to the pioneering work of the 1960s and 1970s and some of which relied on new concepts. The dominant approach in the 1960s was symbolic AI—also called classical AI—which sought to represent human knowledge with a combination of algorithms, language processing, and rules of symbolic logic. Symbolic AI researchers wrote algorithms that enabled computer programs to understand natural language (such as English) and use it to carry out simple tasks such as answering questions. For example, Daniel Bobrow's STUDENT program could solve simple algebra problems written in natural language, and David Warren and Fernando Pereira's CHAT-80 was able to answer geographical questions. Symbolic AI led to a focus on so-called expert systems in the 1980s. An expert system consists of a knowledge base—compiled from interviews with human experts—and a program that enables the computer to use that base intelligently. MYCIN, one of the first expert systems, used several hundred rules about meningitis and bacteremia (bacteria in the blood) to figure out the proper treatment for patients showing signs of either disease.

The other main AI approach was connectionism. This was the idea that thinking is the product of interconnected networks of units called neurons. Connectionism is based on the biological makeup of the human brain. It sees each neuron (or information-carrying cell) in the brain as a digital processor and the brain overall as a kind of computer. Therefore, connectionists seek to reproduce this networking model in machine form. In the late 1960s a book by Marvin Minsky and Seymour Papert discredited the idea of artificial neural networks called perceptrons, claiming their simple input and output processing layers were a dead end. Minsky and Papert, who favored the symbolic AI approach, effectively killed research into neural networks for fifteen years.

WORDS IN CONTEXT

perceptrons
Artificial neural networks that support machine learning.

Yet in the 1980s connectionism revived with a vengeance. In 1986 two psychology professors, David E. Rumelhart and James L. McClelland, published a defense of neural network technology that refuted Minsky and Papert's conclusions. Researchers, frustrated with lack of progress in symbolic AI, flocked to the connectionist camp. They employed powerful new rules of machine learning to train computer networks to use multiple layers of connection. Together with gains in processing speed and memory, the new, more sophisticated focus on neural networks led to major advancements in AI research.

Today the connectionist approach—more often called machine learning or data mining—dominates AI research. In machine learning, the algorithms (or rules) for doing an intelligent task are expressed as complex mathematical functions or statistics and are generated by the computer itself. Human programmers decide what kinds of statistical methods to use and the parameters of the search. One model, called the support vector machine, assigns each new example the computer gathers to one category or another and repeats the process over and over. Another, the so-called decision tree, uses a branching structure to repeatedly generate yes-no decisions from inputs. Each question corresponds to a node or branching point with two possible answers. Each answer then leads to more questions until a task is accomplished or a problem is solved. The connectionist or machine-learning approach essentially trains machines to do things. As computer scientist Jerry Kaplan explains, "Rather than tell the computer *how* to solve the problem, you show it examples of *what* you want it to do."[10]

A World of Data

Machine-learning programs owe much of their success to the vast amounts of data produced in the modern world. Statistics on everything from traffic patterns to shopping preferences are gathered, sifted, compared, and analyzed, enabling computers in effect to

A car driven by Stanley, a robotic software system, crosses the finish line to win DARPA's challenge for self-driving vehicles. To win the competition, the vehicle had to navigate a course in the Mojave Desert, which it accomplished using global positioning and a variety of sensors.

become more intelligent day by day. The idea of neural networks led in the 2000s to cloud computing, the method of storing and processing information over vast computer networks. Using data networks, AI engineers have made many breakthroughs that had long been predicted but had always remained stubbornly out of reach. In 2005 a car driven by Stanley, a Google-designed robot software system, won the Defense Advanced Research Projects Agency (DARPA) Grand Challenge for self-driving vehicles. Stanley employed a Global Positioning System compass and various sensors to navigate a 142-mile (228.5 km) course in the Mojave Desert and finish ahead of all challengers. Another breakthrough familiar to smartphone users is speech recognition, which enables a person to ask questions to a computer app, such as Apple's Siri. In 2015 Google announced it had achieved an error rate on speech recognition of only 8 percent. The company has also developed an app for recognizing objects and images—a computer skill demonstrated by recognizing cats in YouTube videos.

In 2005 the futurist and inventor Ray Kurzweil made a startling prediction about AI. Kurzweil said that by 2045 the intelligence of artificial minds would exceed that of the human brain, a development that he calls the Singularity. But long before anything like the Singularity even becomes possible, AI is certain to play an increasingly large role in people's daily lives. Science writer Kevin Kelly, like Kurzweil an optimist about AI, figures the technology will not rule over humanity or meld with it but become simply a very important tool that adds IQ to almost everything. According to Kelly:

> The AI on the horizon looks more like Amazon Web Services—cheap, reliable, industrial-grade digital smartness running behind everything, and almost invisible except when it blinks off. This common utility will serve you as much IQ as you want but no more than you need. Like all utilities, AI will be supremely boring, even as it transforms the Internet, the global economy, and civilization. . . . In fact, the business plans of the next 10,000 startups are easy to forecast: Take X and add AI. This is a big deal and now it's here.[11]

Chapter 2

Speeding into Business and Marketing

The US stock market makes baffling moves sometimes, but this was ridiculous. On May 6, 2010, the Dow Jones Industrial Average plunged nearly 1,000 points in thirty minutes, wiping out $1 trillion in value from household-name companies like General Electric. The market quickly recovered, however, closing down only 3 percent after a drop of almost 9 percent. The incident became known as the Flash Crash. US government investigators traced the sudden crash to a computerized selling program that employed AI technology. A small firm based in Shawnee Mission, Kansas, was blamed for using a trading algorithm with a design flaw, causing a feedback loop when it interacted with other high-speed automatic trading programs. An already stressed stock market responded by selling off rapidly, causing the crash.

In April 2015 Navinder Singh Sarao, a computer trader working from his parents' home in London, England, was arrested for allegedly playing a role in the crash. Using a software program he had modified himself, Sarao had "spoofed" the market by offering and then withdrawing fake sell orders totaling billions of dollars. According to Michael Greenberger, a former regulator at the US Commodity Futures Trading Commission, "This was a world-wide threat to economic well-being, and it only lasted a matter of minutes."[12]

Dangers of Automatic Stock Trading Platforms

The 2010 Flash Crash emphasized an aspect of today's stock market little known to those outside the financial industry: Most trading is done not only on computers but also by computers. This is accomplished with high-frequency trading (HFT) software platforms, also known as quantitative trading, or quants. Like all stock traders, the platforms seek to buy low and sell high. In the two seconds it takes a savvy human trader to punch a key and buy or sell a stock, an HFT platform can complete up to one hundred thousand trades, each measured in milliseconds.

But the computer's advantage is not only its speedy trading. It also has the AI-related ability to analyze multiple exchanges almost instantaneously in search of discrepancies in pricing, in which one exchange offers a stock at a lower price than others. When the AI program detects an opportunity, it pounces—without waiting for a human decision. In a fraction of a second, it can buy and sell huge blocks of shares repeatedly, before the divergence in prices goes away. In fact, by identifying these discrepancies, the rapid-fire computer trading actually helps bring the pricing back into line. Meanwhile, the average investor's order of one hundred shares, entered on a home computer, gets overwhelmed in the tidal waves of computer trading taking place at any given time. Some have suggested that market officials should level the playing field by creating a delay of one second for all trades, which would mostly eliminate the AI platform's advantages in speed. However, since the exchanges make their money from the number of trades transacted, this is unlikely to happen anytime soon.

> **WORDS IN CONTEXT**
>
> **quantitative trading**
> Stock trading strategies that depend on complex computations and number crunching to identify opportunities in the stock market.

The real problem comes when lots of superfast trading programs interact. During the 2010 Flash Crash, a sudden drop in stock prices triggered so-called stop-loss orders to sell at any price. As the selling mounted, safety alarms set to protect against losses went off in the HFT computer programs, and they began

In the past, the floor of the New York Stock Exchange (pictured) was routinely crowded with traders, but today, most of the trading is performed by computers running high-frequency trading software. Such software platforms can complete up to 50,000 trades per second.

dumping shares at a furious pace. The unprecedented number of trades overwhelmed the system, creating wild price spreads that the HFT algorithms then mistook as opportunities for further trading. The system became flooded with false information. Apple's stock momentarily skyrocketed to $100,000 a share, while other large companies fell to pennies a share. Finally the Chicago Mercantile Exchange, a smaller competitor to the big New York markets, called a halt to trading for five seconds. This breathing space enabled the HFT programs to reset, which helped return pricing to normal.

The Next Generation of Digital Trading Programs

HFT programs are nothing new. The idea dates back to the 1980s and research among some small tech firms and the world's largest banks. But those trading platforms used AI to accomplish specific objectives set by human programmers. The next generation of trading programs seeks to use so-called deep learning to enable a machine to make its own investment decisions. Deep learning involves training a large neural network to recognize patterns in data. One trading robot that employs deep learning is the work of a team of robotic engineers, mathematicians, and ex-bankers at the Hong Kong–based trading firm Aidyia. The team has spent three years and millions of dollars developing a computerized investor that can teach itself to adapt to changing conditions in the stock market, with no guidance from human handlers.

Father of High-Frequency Trading

The origins of HFT in the stock market remain shadowy to this day. Several traders and computer experts take credit for the idea. One person whose role is indisputable is David Whitcomb. A mild-mannered former finance professor, Whitcomb was struck by the failure of human market makers—experts who fill stock orders on the exchange floor— during the Black Monday crash of October 19, 1987. As the stock market plunged, no one seemed able to establish a so-called bottom—a baseline price from which stocks could rebound. Whitcomb thought computers could do a better job of buying and selling stocks for clients and bringing order when necessary to a chaotic market.

Acting on his notion, Whitcomb contacted James Hawkes, a statistician and former student living in Mount Pleasant, South Carolina. Hawkes helped round up a team of computer and math experts. Together they formed a company called Mount Pleasant in 1988, later changing the name to Automated Trading Desk. The company's AI-based platforms tracked various factors that impact stocks and made lightning-fast calculations about stock price movements. The computers were able to trade stocks much faster than any human. So successful was the firm that Citigroup paid $700 million for it in 2007. As for Whitcomb, he became a trusted source for advice about computer-based trading on Wall Street. He also insisted, in his quiet way, that he was the real inventor of HFT. Today he maintains with pride, "Automated Trading Desk was the first of the high frequency trading firms."

Quoted in Stephen Gandel, "Unmasking the Father of High Frequency Trading," *Fortune*, June 10, 2014. www .fortune.com.

Today's smartphone apps like the one pictured here enable users to monitor stock exchange activity. A German company is developing an app that will employ market sentiment on social media sites such as Facebook and Twitter to aid users in making trading decisions.

The trading robot combs through mountains of data, in both numbers and words, to create its own unique strategies. According to Ben Goertzel, Aidyia's cofounder and chief scientist, "It's seeing patterns that aren't easy for the human mind to wrap itself around."[13] For example, the robot might analyze the trading history of millions of online stock traders to identify the best strategies and combine them to adapt itself into a super trader. Or it might notice a spike in the number of prepaid cell phone cards purchased in certain African nations and connect that fact to the potential size of the coming harvest. African farmers are likely to spend more on phone cards when they expect larger crop yields and an increase in phone negotiations with buyers. With such rapid-fire insights, computerized trading programs could one day replace human traders. "The human mind has many strengths, but ultimately lacks the memory, calculation capability and breadth of information integration to keep up with AI systems in the context of analyzing, understanding and predicting modern financial markets," says Goertzel. "In the end it's going to be viewed as irresponsible to entrust trillions of dollars to some emotional human being."[14]

The new AI trading programs are not just for market experts. The German company Neokami is developing an app to help ordinary investors compete with high-powered hedge funds. Neokami's platform uses AI to sift through data and predict the price movement of stocks and commodities over various time periods. The data it employs include not only expert analysis and stock price history but also variables like market sentiment on Twitter and Facebook. Investors can then set their trading strategies based on the app's predictions. "We would be using the same algorithms used by the world's top tech companies for things like image recognition (and) computer learning but apply that to stock markets," says Ozel Christo, founder and CEO of Neokami. "We can analyze millions of variables within seconds and create a customized predictive model for any stock."[15] Christo foresees that, depending on the time frame a user is seeking, the app could be 75 percent to 95 percent accurate in predicting stock price movement. Although experts remain cautious regarding such claims, there is no denying the financial industry's interest in AI. Sentient Technologies, another AI-based finance company, recently raised $103 million for its fledgling business.

AI Systems in the Business World

Aside from the stock market, AI systems are also making inroads in the business world. In late 2014 Royal Dutch Shell and Baker Hughes, two large companies in the oil and gas field, began testing a new AI platform for office work called Amelia. Named for aviation pioneer Amelia Earhart, Amelia is a cognitive knowledge worker created by New York–based IPSoft. So far Amelia, like an entry-level worker, is being tested on accounts payable in the companies' customer service departments. But Amelia's developers say this only hints at the platform's real capabilities, such as supporting oil-rig operations. "For example, an engineer could interact with Amelia in order to speed up diagnosis and resolution of problems with machinery,"[16] says IPSoft spokesperson Sean

Rocket Fuel for Online Advertising

AI-based programmatic advertising is the marketing wave of the future. Programmatic ads target specific audiences and demographics automatically, thereby giving advertisers more value for their advertising dollars. For example, a company might use this approach to reach men in the Pacific Northwest aged eighteen to thirty-five who enjoy mountain biking. Once identified using AI platforms, these individuals would see displays of the company's ads each time they visited their favorite websites. Marketing experts predict that by 2018, more than half of all digital advertising will be programmatic.

As the field of programmatic advertising becomes more crowded, there is fierce competition for ad space online. Companies jostle for space through a process called real-time bidding. In the time it takes for a page to load in a user's web browser, information about the page and the user speeds to an ad exchange. There the space is auctioned off automatically to the advertiser willing to make the highest bid. That company's ad is then loaded into the web page almost instantly, with the whole process completed in milliseconds. Digital marketing firms like the aptly named Rocket Fuel strive to bring new efficiency to this hectic bidding process. Rocket Fuel uses machine learning and big data to help its clients thrive in the world of digital advertising. According to CEO George John, "Now with ad exchanges, marketers have the ability to use data to identify individuals with demonstrated human intention, planet wide, with well over 50 billion opportunities every day."

Quoted in Bruce Rogers, "Rocket Fuel Brings Artificial Intelligence to Marketing Effectiveness," *Forbes*, February 4, 2015. www.forbes.com.

McIlrath. Baker Hughes, which provides a variety of oil field services, is training Amelia to interact with the company's thousands of suppliers and answer questions about invoices and inventory. Baker Hughes executives believe Amelia could save company employees thousands of work hours, allowing them to concentrate on less tedious matters.

Amelia's potential is not limited to the oil and gas industry. Once installed in a company's call center, she can use her intelligence algorithms to absorb instruction manuals and guidelines in a matter of seconds. (IPSoft personnel always refer to Amelia using the feminine pronoun.) By contrast, human staffers can require weeks or even months to master these materials. It is Amelia's ability to process natural language—she "speaks" more than twenty languages—and comprehend difficult problems that sets the platform apart from other advanced AI systems like IBM's Watson. She can grasp the meaning of customer queries in e-mails and phone calls and use logic to connect concepts. When she discovers what is needed, she either takes steps to resolve the issue herself or scans the Internet or company network for relevant information. Only as a last resort does Amelia send a case to a human expert—and even then she will monitor the response and file it away for future reference. "Amelia learns with every transaction and builds a mind map on the fly," says IPSoft CEO Chetan Dube. "As more incidents come in, this mind map is rapidly building, just the way humans build their mind maps. Soon it represents the cumulative intellect of all the different [employees] who have been fielding these different calls."[17]

With her wide-ranging abilities, Amelia has everything it takes to become a highly prized worker. Yet AI systems like Amelia could also transform the global workforce in less positive ways. Instead of freeing employees to do more creative tasks, the new machines might simply put large numbers of people out of work. Many experts worry about AI eliminating jobs faster than it can create new ones. For example, law firms could use Amelia to replace legal aides and interns. "I already talked to one big law firm and they said they're not hiring as many of those sorts of people," says Erik Brynjolfsson, an economist at MIT, "because a machine can scan through hundreds of thousands or millions of documents and find the relevant information for a case or a trial much more quickly and accurately than a human can."[18] UK economists Carl Benedikt Frey and Michael A. Osborne estimate that 47 percent of American jobs are at high risk of being lost to automation in a decade or two.

What the Computer Knows About Its Users

Whether at work or at home, most people spend hours on their PCs, tablets, or cell phones. What they may not realize is that while they are reading their computer screens, the computer essentially is reading them. Websites not only provide information and services, they also collect data about the user. This data can include personal information such as name, address, phone numbers, and Social Security number; names of family members and friends; credit history; shopping preferences; political leanings; and even current location. AI programs track a person's browsing history through browser-based technologies such as cookies, which are small packets of data specific to a particular user and website. Cookies enable the server to deliver web pages tailored to a user's history. That is why a person who has recently shopped for jeans online will see jeans ads popping up on various sites. An AI program finds out what a person likes—what books, movies, clothes, cars, vacations, and so forth—and then automatically tries to interest that person in making a purchase. The search engine company Google collects such a vast amount of information about its customers that it has faced a backlash based on concerns about privacy. To ease these concerns, Google has created a hub called My Account, where users can examine their account settings and view what information Google is collecting about them.

Helping Users Get Better Results

As computers get smarter, they can also help users get faster results and even overcome their own mistakes. In 2010 Google introduced a search tool called Google Instant that uses AI to guess what a person is searching for as he or she types keywords into a search box. According to the company, Google Instant can save users two to five seconds per search. In 2014 Google updated its search algorithms with Hummingbird, an AI program that uses synonyms and context to improve search results. Hummingbird makes logical inferences about a user's probable intent. For example, when a user enters the word "weather," he or she is probably seeking a forecast, not a discussion of meteorology.

The company that produces the search engine Google (pictured) has updated the technology several times using AI. These programs guess what a person is searching for when entering keywords and make logical inferences about a user's intent in order to improve search results.

Another innovation is an AI system known as RankBrain, which Google introduced in October 2015. RankBrain uses machine learning to make educated guesses about unusual or poorly phrased search queries. If it sees a word or phrase it does not recognize, it refers to its own huge stores of written language to find words or phrases with a similar meaning. This allows it to suggest search results more likely to satisfy the user's needs. RankBrain is only one of hundreds of signals that make up an algorithm that decides what results appear on a Google search page and how they are ranked. Yet within its first few months, it became the third-most important signal contributing to Google's search query results. "The other signals, they're all based on discoveries and insights that people in information retrieval had had, but there's no learning,"[19] notes Greg Corrado, a senior research scientist at Google. As Andrew Howlett, chief technology officer of a major marketing firm, explains:

> Customers providing reviews use real language and say it in ways that people might also ask a question through Google. For example, in a [restaurant] review, someone might say, "This place has the best chips and salsa anywhere that doesn't cost a fortune." That sentence will help now with someone searching for something like, "I'm on a budget, where's a good restaurant with awesome chips and salsa?"[20]

RankBrain continually files away such information for the future. As it learns, it can help make sense out of other garbled queries—in effect making the user that much smarter.

Marketing on the Run

Increasingly, artificial intelligence platforms seek to manage a person's total shopping experience. These platforms soak up reams of data about each customer as part of a constant marketing effort. A Seattle technology company recently launched Mona, an AI-based app that serves as a personal shopping assistant. Mona is like an expert store clerk who knows the customer well and communicates by cell phone. If a user wants to know when a new style of handbag goes on sale, Mona has the information. If a user wants a winter coat for less than seventy-five dollars, Mona offers plenty of suggestions. If the best options are not in local stores but online, Mona knows that too. And the more a person interacts with Mona, the more the software program learns about the person's size, style, budget, favorite colors, and preferred retailers. Users can even link their e-mail accounts with Mona so that the app can pick up further marketing hints. Mona cofounder and CEO Orkun Atik explains:

> This is our first step towards creating a mobile shopping experience that is similar to an in-store dialogue between a customer and assistant. . . . We're using machine learning

to analyze millions of products every day and build a product intelligence graph. . . . We have a personalization engine that learns [the] user's past purchases, behavior and feedback and builds [a] digital model of [the] user across all stores and categories.[21]

One thing Mona cannot do, however, is share a latte after a long day of shopping.

With customers today expecting more choices and personalized service, AI platforms for marketing and sales are certain to expand. Companies like Google, Apple, Facebook, and Amazon are seeking to make machine learning a vital part of people's everyday lives. Although machines are still a long way from being able to apply knowledge as humans do, they already can help people make smarter, faster decisions that lead—most of the time—to better outcomes.

Chapter 3

Doctors in a Box

As a savvy dermatologist in Long Island, New York, Kavita Mariwalla has treated all sorts of skin cancers, rashes, and boils. But when a patient showed up with bullous pemphigoid, a rare and potentially disfiguring skin condition that erupts in large, watery blisters, Mariwalla was perplexed. The medication usually prescribed for the autoimmune disorder was unavailable. Mariwalla turned to her computer and a medical-information site called Modernizing Medicine. Seconds later she had the name of another drug that had proved successful in similar cases. The drug subsequently helped her patient recover.

The site's AI-based system enabled her to access the collected knowledge of more than thirty-seven hundred medical professionals and information from more than 14 million patient visits, in addition to details on treating patients with related profiles. Like Amazon's website, which uses a massive store of consumer data to suggest relevant purchases, sites like Modernizing Medicine tap into troves of medical data to offer possible treatments. "It gives you access to data, and data is king," says Mariwalla. "It's been very helpful, especially in clinically challenging situations."[22]

AI and Electronic Health Records

Mariwalla's experience is typical of how artificial intelligence is transforming modern medicine. The ability of AI and its complex algorithms to crunch huge amounts of data and find underlying patterns is proving to be a valuable clinical tool for doctors and hospitals. The rise of AI platforms coincides with the expansion of electronic medical records. Unlike paper records, the electronic versions not only provide helpful details about patient histories and treatments but also make this information digitally searchable

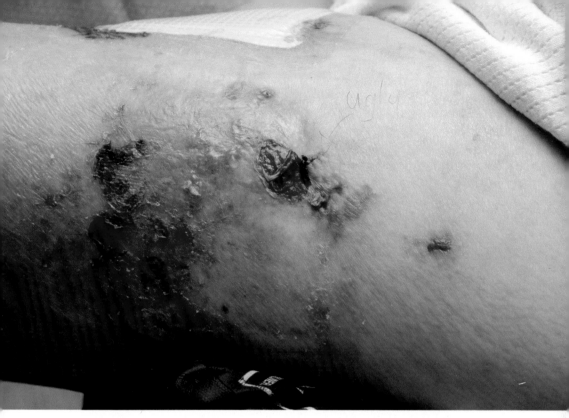

Dr. Kavita Mariwalla, a Long Island dermatologist, consulted Modernizing Medicine, a website containing medical information, to assist her in treating a patient with skin blisters like the ones pictured here. Tools such as this employ AI to sift through vast amounts of data and detect patterns that can aid clinicians in diagnosing and treating medical disorders.

and thus of more practical use to AI systems. "Electronic health records [are] like large quarries where there's lots of gold, and we're just beginning to mine them,"[23] says Dr. Eric Horvitz, managing director of Microsoft Research's Redmond Lab and an expert on applying AI in health care settings. Moreover, there has been a push under 2010's Affordable Care Act to employ new technologies for improved outcomes and cost savings. This, along with the advent of cheaper, more powerful computers, promises a new age of digital medicine.

Already doctors and hospitals are using computer networks and AI platforms to search patient records for risks of heart disease, kidney failure, or postoperative infections. Monitoring treatment data can reduce the need for hospital readmissions, a cost-saving emphasis of health care reform. And AI systems today are able to combine patients' health data—including genetic profiles—with materials held in public databases, online textbooks, and medical journals to offer strategies for targeted treatment.

Some doctors are setting up their own AI-based systems to monitor patient care automatically. At Vanderbilt University Medical Center in Nashville, Tennessee, doctors receive pop-up notifications as part of a patient's electronic medical records. Should a patient be allergic to a certain drug or unlikely to benefit from it because of genetic traits, a bright yellow alert message will flash on the doctor's tablet or computer screen. The Vanderbilt system will then suggest an alternative medication. Doctors at Vanderbilt say they follow the computer's advice about two-thirds of the time, and they admit that the AI system is often better than their intuition.

For now, computerized health care systems are best at combing through information in neat categories. This data is usually found in billing codes, lab test results, and lists of medications. The systems are less successful at dealing with so-called unstructured data such as X-rays and doctors' notes about patient care. Analyzing these requires image- and language-recognition skills that computers have been slow to develop. Nonetheless, they are making strides. Soon an AI program might discern from a doctor's notes—describing a patient's stained fingers and shortness of breath—that the patient is a smoker, despite assertions to the contrary.

Beginnings of AI in Medicine

The idea of using artificially intelligent computers for medical diagnoses dates to 1959. In that year radiology professor Robert S. Ledley and his colleague Lee B. Lusted published an influential article on the use of digital computers in medicine. "Reasoning Foundations of Medical Diagnosis" appeared in *Science* magazine and caused a sensation in the medical field. Ledley and Lusted envisioned the use of large databases to help doctors share vital information and make better diagnoses. Their hope was that computer systems would become like so-called doctors in a box—a handy diagnostic tool drawing on vast amounts of data and making use of computerized logic and probability. In the article, Ledley and Lusted linked the complex math of computer science with

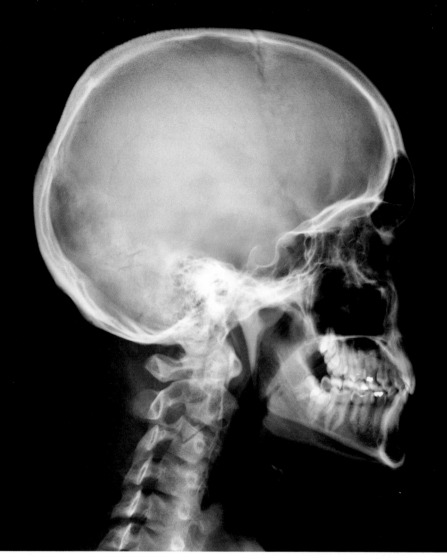

Although computerized health care systems function well when analyzing easily categorized information such as billing codes and lab results, they are less successful when dealing with so-called unstructured data such as X-rays, like the one of a human head pictured here.

their own expertise on diagnostic medicine to show how the two disciplines could work together. The authors also admitted that computers could not replace human doctors completely:

> The mathematical techniques that we have discussed and the associated use of computers are intended to be an aid to the physician. This method in no way implies that a computer can take over the physician's duties. Quite the

A Rule-Based Program for Treating Infections

One of the first examples of AI in medicine was MYCIN, a so-called expert system for treating blood infections. An expert system is a computer program that uses artificial intelligence to solve problems within a specialized area that usually calls for human expertise. Work on MYCIN began in 1972 at Stanford University in Palo Alto, California. Edward Shortliffe, a Canadian-born physician and computer scientist, led the research team that developed the program. MYCIN was designed to use a knowledge base of more than six hundred if-then rules to identify bacteria that cause dangerous infections such as bacteremia and meningitis. Then by way of a reasoning strategy, it would suggest appropriate antibiotics for treatment. The program's name referred to the suffix -*mycin* that appears in the names of many antibiotics.

Although doctors never actually used MYCIN to make treatment decisions, research at Stanford Medical School showed the program's recommendations for treating infections to be basically correct in almost 70 percent of cases. With this success rate, MYCIN actually outperformed faculty members at Stanford's medical school. The main drawback to MYCIN was its inability to integrate with other data systems. At the time it was invented, there were no personal computers or electronic medical records to support the program. Data about individual patients had to be entered into the MYCIN system, a time-consuming process. Nonetheless, MYCIN demonstrated that a rule-based computer system could play an important role in helping physicians make informed clinical decisions for treatment.

reverse; it implies that the physician's task may become more complicated. . . . However, the benefit that we hope may be gained to offset these increased difficulties is the ability to make a more precise diagnosis and a more scientific determination of the treatment plan.[24]

Researchers in the 1960s, building on Ledley and Lusted's ideas, began looking into diagnosing diseases by applying Bayes' theorem. This is a formula that relates the probability of a disease being present to the error rates of tests used to diagnose it. The Bayes' theorem approach seemed promising, but soon it was shown to have serious flaws. These included a need for data that often was not available and an inability to diagnose multiple diseases occurring simultaneously in the same patient.

By the 1980s research on AI in medicine had begun to stall, as predictions about the technology's success proved to be premature. Some health care professionals questioned the wisdom of relying on a computer for complicated decisions about medical care. Experts warned that busy doctors would be reluctant to spend time learning a new system, however promising. In the 1990s the emphasis in AI medical research changed from diagnosis of disease to support for health care workers engaged in patient care. AI systems were thought to be best suited for generating alerts and reminders about fairly routine matters, such as changes in a patient's condition, lab test results, and drug orders—sort of a digitized office assistant.

In the past twenty years, however, the expanded use of electronic medical records—and thus of usable data—has raised exciting new possibilities for AI in medicine. Improvements in how computers recognize images and natural language have also helped advance the technology. Research once again is focused on integrating AI into hospitals and clinics for everything from diagnosis to disease management and patient care. In 2009, for example, General Electric created a software program that could suggest treatment options in real time during patient visits by recognizing patterns in data. In addition, software engineering firms like Artificial Intelligence in Medicine are developing an array of health care products that use informatics, which is the science of processing data for storage and retrieval. Today the concept of doctors in a box is much closer to becoming reality.

Using Computers to Reduce Medical Errors

One area in which the doctors in a box concept could have the greatest effect is in preventing medical errors. In 2014 a Senate

Medical Care by Mobile Phone

When a person needs a doctor's expertise at his or her fingertips, there is an app for that. Several companies in the United States and United Kingdom are developing AI-based digital health applications for mobile phones and tablets. Services like HealthTap, Push Doctor, and Babylon Health incorporate AI to check users' medical history and pinpoint their ailments. Britain's Babylon Health is the least expensive of these mobile apps, charging users five pounds (about eight dollars) a month to talk to a general practitioner whenever they choose without limits. The app's one hundred full-time physicians can write prescriptions, schedule follow-ups, and refer users to specialists. In only two years, Babylon Health has built an active user base of more than 250,000, half of whom get the service through their employer.

Like the other apps for video consultations, Babylon Health uses AI to screen patients for a virtual appointment. An automated female voice asks a series of questions to determine the user's symptoms. The system is unfailingly polite; when told that the user has a headache, for example, it responds: "I'm sorry to hear that." The AI program can calculate symptoms and decide if an appointment is necessary at lightning speed, thus saving time and money for Babylon Health's physicians. "It would have taken a doctor five minutes to ask these questions," says Ali Parsa, founder and CEO of Babylon Health, noting that the app might spend only one minute. "We're doing with healthcare what Google did with information. Making it available to everyone with prices people can afford."

Quoted in Parmy Olson, "The A.I. Will See You Now," *Forbes*, November 12, 2015. www.forbes.com.

hearing on health care safety disclosed that medical error was the third-most frequent cause of death in the United States behind heart disease and cancer, resulting in about four hundred thousand deaths annually. According to *Healthcare IT News*, preventable medical errors cost the country as much as $1 trillion per year. Medical errors lead to thousands of complications every day. Errors in diagnosis alone affect 12 million patients a year.

Computer experts see these figures as a huge opportunity for AI-based medicine. Although some errors are caused by procedural mistakes or accidents, a large percentage occur due to incomplete or incorrect information about the patient's history or condition. Again, an important key is maintaining complete electronic health records and ensuring they are available whenever a patient seeks treatment. This can prevent errors due to a patient's faulty memory or inability to communicate. But AI initiatives also can address a physician's occasional failings. Science writer Christopher de la Torre notes:

> Drawing on millions of points of data, smart software can think of things doctors forget. And while human doctors become fatigued, their AI counterparts remain alert 24 hours a day, 7 days a week, even as patient waiting rooms ebb and flow. It's a logical partnership—one that will allow doctors to concentrate on solving medical problems while their artificial assistants crunch data.[25]

In 2009, for example, the Mayo Clinic in Rochester, Minnesota, began testing a so-called artificial neural network (ANN) to correct the misdiagnosis of patients previously thought to have endocarditis, a deadly heart infection. The ANN is a new type of teachable software that mimics the brain's cognitive functions by using computer network connections, enabling it to react to situations based on its accumulated knowledge. Researchers at the Mayo Clinic put the ANN software through three separate training periods, presenting it with as many different scenarios as possible. The goal was to teach the software to recognize endocarditis in patients with implanted heart devices— and also to recognize when it is not present. Because the mortality rate for endocarditis approaches one in five, and diagnosis of the heart infection usually results in a very invasive procedure—insertion of a probe down the patient's throat— the stakes are high to get the diagnosis right.

To test the software, researchers presented it with the data from 189 former Mayo Clinic patients who had been diagnosed with heart implant–related endocarditis, almost one-fourth of them incorrectly. The ANN program made the correct judgment in 99 percent of the cases. With this success rate, physicians are more likely to rely on the software's input. "In some cases, [ANN] might enable us to correctly diagnose patients without performing [the esophagus probe] or to select patients who might benefit from additional testing," says Dr. M. Rizwan Sohail, the lead author of the study. "The result would be reduced healthcare costs and improved outcomes."[26]

Crunching Millions of Data Points

A crucial test for improved outcomes in modern medicine is cancer treatment. Here too AI platforms are starting to make an impact. Researchers at MIT's Computer Science and Artificial Intelligence Laboratory have developed a computer program that uses its learning from thousands of past pathology reports to automatically suggest cancer diagnoses and treatments. MIT professor Peter Szolovits and PhD student Yuan Luo, working alongside physicians from Massachusetts General Hospital, focused their research on the three most prevalent subtypes of lymphoma, a common form of cancer that affects the immune system.

Lymphoma has more than fifty distinct subtypes that are usually hard to distinguish from one another. Experts say that as many as 15 percent of lymphoma cases are initially misdiagnosed or misclassified. This can lead to significant problems, since different types of lymphoma call for radically different treatments. If a patient is misdiagnosed as having an incurable form of lymphoma, his or her disease might go untreated, thus putting the patient's life at risk. In addition, classifying lymphomas has long been a source of controversy among pathologists, or physicians who examine tissues for diagnosis and treatment. In 2008 the World Health Organization revised its guidelines for lymphoma classification, in effect confirming how subtle the differences can be. Diagnosing lymphoma is a sizable challenge for human doctors, let alone a computer program.

WORDS IN CONTEXT

lymphoma
Blood cancer that arises in the cells of the body's immune system.

Nonetheless, the MIT platform shows tremendous promise. It taps into the medical archives of large hospitals and institutions to make use of millions of data points about lymphoma treatments. Luo has devised a technique that organizes the data into a three-dimensional table, a format that allows the data to be grouped in clusters for easier comparison of test results. Szolovits believes that Luo's work, when applied to vast data sets, can help doctors understand the range of lymphomas and how they relate to each other. "Our ultimate goal is to be able to focus these techniques on extremely large amounts of lymphoma data, on the order of millions of cases," says Szolovits. "If we can do that, and identify the features that are specific to different subtypes, then we'd go a long way towards making doctors' jobs easier—and, maybe, patients' lives longer."[27]

Watson and Deep Learning in Medicine

IBM's Watson is now being used to help doctors diagnose diseases with more speed and accuracy. Researchers at IBM are improving the AI platform's ability to use its sophisticated computer vision to process enormous stores of medical images. This innovation is powered by the technology of deep learning, an approach to AI based on neural networks in the human brain. Deep learning teaches computers to discern patterns in data, enabling them to recognize speech and images with amazing precision. Now IBM's technicians believe Watson is ready to make a major leap into the medical field, where it can process the 90 percent of clinical data that is stored as images. In August 2015 IBM announced it was buying Merge Healthcare, a company with a data set of some 30 billion medical images. The purchase, one of IBM's three recent acquisitions of data-based health care companies, is part of a strategy to draw on a variety of data sources, including images and text-based medical records, to assist doctors in making decisions for treatment.

For now the most promising area for Watson's automated image processing is in detecting melanoma, a type of skin cancer. Because there is so much variation in the way it appears in different patients, melanoma is notoriously difficult to diagnose. By

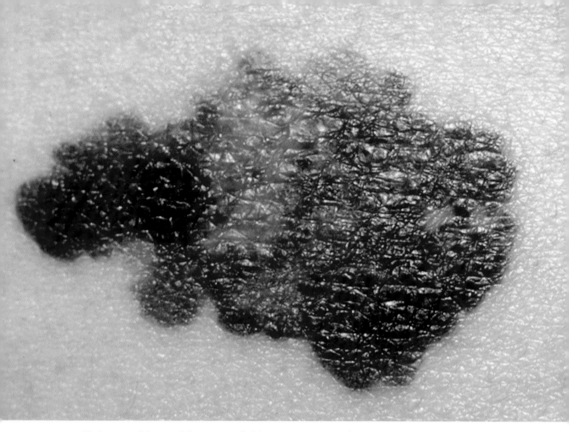

Melanoma (pictured) is a type of skin cancer that is difficult to diagnose because it varies so much from patient to patient. Researchers hope that computers can assist humans in this task by comparing millions of images of melanomas and learning to identify the subtle features of each type.

feeding Watson millions of images of melanoma, it is hoped that the system will learn to distinguish subtle but crucial features of the disease. According to technology writer Mike Orcutt, "The technology IBM envisions might be able to compare a new image from a patient with many others in a database and then rapidly give the doctor important information, gleaned from the images as well as from text-based records, about the diagnosis and potential treatments."[28] Researchers believe Watson could soon do something similar by searching for early signs of tumors in computed tomography lung scans.

Another possible medical use for Watson is matching brain cancer mutations to cancer drugs best suited to treat them. Today doctors must first sequence the DNA in a tumor several times, then search through billions of data points to find how the cancer cell differs from a normal cell. Finally, doctors must determine which of thousands of mutations are the most important ones to target. Watson has the ability to scan those thousands of DNA mutations very rapidly, helping physicians pinpoint a personalized cancer treatment for each patient's tumor. The practice could save cancer clinics enormous amounts of time and money while also delivering improved care. "What we currently do is essentially go through the mutations by hand with a team of doctors. . . . One by one, we're trying to connect up which mutations might match which drugs," says Bob Darnell, CEO and scientific director at New York Genome Center. "Rather than trying to do all of this informatics by hand, Watson can be used, instead of winning at *Jeopardy!*, to beat cancer."[29]

Watson is one of the most promising examples of the doctors in a box concept at work. As more medical records are digitized and placed in online networks, such programs can provide huge benefits to patients in the doctor's office, the laboratory, and the operating room.

Chapter 4

Smarter and Safer Travel

Safe, efficient travel is a priority for today's computer scientists and engineers. New cars today are equipped with the latest sensors and onboard computers to make traveling proceed more smoothly. Yet drivers of these cars often sit frustrated at an old-fashioned red light with no vehicles in view in either direction. Smart cars call for smart traffic lights—at least that is the thinking of Samah El-Tantawy, an engineer at the Toronto Intelligent Transportation Systems Centre. El-Tantawy has come up with a traffic light system that makes use of AI and game theory to cut the average wait time at an intersection by 40 percent. She claims that with her system a commute through thirty intersections could be shaved by more than twelve minutes. Adding together morning and evening drives, the savings—both in time and frustration—are significant.

> ## WORDS IN CONTEXT
>
> **game theory**
> A theory that deals with mathematical models of conflict and cooperation among intelligent players or decision makers.

A Decentralized Approach

The problem, says El-Tantawy, is that most traffic lights at intersections today operate according to preprogrammed cycles that proceed with little or no input from the actual fluctuations in traffic. Sensors placed in pavements along major streets usually extend a green light when a longer period is needed to keep traffic flowing. With El-Tantawy's system, video cameras, data inputs from vehicles (if available), computer chips, and digital routers combine to analyze how many drivers are sailing through intersections and how many are halted at a red light for no particular reason.

Traffic halts at a red light in New York City. Most traffic lights today operate according to preprogrammed schedules that do not take traffic flow into account, but future systems will prompt lights to change based on the actual number of cars present.

The system—called MARLIN for Multi-Agent Reinforcement Learning for Integrated Network—aims cameras in all four directions at each intersection and keeps track of input not only from main thoroughfares but feeder streets as well. "Our approach is decentralized, where the intelligence or math to assign the greens is done on the fly at each intersection," says El-Tantawy. "The brain sits at each intersection, and calculates the best timing to minimize the number of cars approaching and waiting, and it coordinates those decisions with other lights at other intersections."[30]

In other words, the traffic lights learn how to keep traffic moving at an optimal pace. MARLIN notes the so-called queue lengths—the number of cars at each red light—and the delay times to the next green light and adjusts each neighboring intersection so that motorists and pedestrians wait for as brief a period as possible. Unlike the old, rigid system that relied on outdated guesses about traffic patterns, MARLIN is able to adapt to new patterns as they arise. El-Tantawy and her fellow engineers admit that MARLIN is only one tool in addressing inner-city gridlock. Delays can also be caused by bad weather, road construction, lane closures, accidents, and other unforeseen circumstances. Still, MARLIN demonstrates that smarter traffic lights can minimize delays for everyone.

Smarter, More Intuitive Cars

As traffic lights get smarter, so too do automobiles. Automakers worldwide are turning to AI technology to make smarter, more intuitive cars. In September 2015 Toyota Motor Corporation announced a five-year, $50 million joint research project with MIT and Stanford University to make cars that are better able to avoid collisions. Toyota wants its researchers to design AI-based software that can identify objects in various road environments, make correct driving decisions, and coordinate instantaneously not only with the driver, but also with passengers, pedestrians, and other vehicles. To help with its AI initiative, Toyota also hired Gill Pratt. Pratt is a robotics expert from DARPA, a division of the Pentagon involved in creating self-driving cars, among many other endeavors. Like other car companies, Toyota expects future automobiles to be more like digital devices that interact over networks than traditional self-sufficient vehicles.

WORDS IN CONTEXT

decentralized
Redistributed or spread away from a central hub.

One key statistic that drives the development of smart cars is the average number of traffic fatalities in the United States each day: 110. To address this problem, MIT scientists have modeled human driving behavior to develop algorithms for computerized cars. They seek to combine human driving patterns with electronic safety systems to help prevent crashes. The safety systems include automated cruise control to regulate speed, radar- or laser-based sensors that slow the vehicle when it approaches other cars, blind-spot warning systems that alert the driver with lights or beeps when there is another car present that the driver cannot see, and traction control systems that apply the brakes automatically if skidding or lost steering control is detected.

Analysis of driving patterns includes data about drivers' tendencies, such as where they tend to accelerate (on-ramps and lane changes) or decelerate (off-ramps and intersections). These patterns, when filtered through an algorithm, enable the vehicle's intelligent transportation system (ITS) to figure out where the vehicle is probably heading next. The ITS calculations are continuously weighed against data from onboard sensors about the positions of surrounding cars. The vehicle with ITS senses at once where and how it could theoretically collide with another car—called the capture set—and acts to avoid those danger zones where risk of a crash is heightened.

In recent tests on a closed track with non-ITS cars, the ITS-equipped vehicle was able to avoid the capture set ninety-seven times out of one hundred. In the three capture-set scenarios,

Flocking to Waze

Drivers in Israel are not known for their patience. They change lanes compulsively and do not spare the horn with slower drivers. But Israeli drivers are improving their road relations by adopting Waze, a satellite navigation system for smartphones. The popular app helps drivers cope with road hazards, traffic jams, and speed traps by not only giving them directions but also enabling them to work together. Its verbal directions—voice options include actor Morgan Freeman and an Elvis imitator, plus various languages—rely on real-time data about traffic and road conditions, much of it culled from other users. This form of crowdsourcing creates a networking effect. By tracking each phone as it travels, Waze's AI processors can analyze data for speed, traffic flow, and optimal routes. The app has led many Waze users to think of themselves as a community. "One of the features is that you can see and talk to other Wazers," says Issamar Ginzberg, a business consultant and rabbi. "It's very interactive."

Waze is the invention of Ehud Shabtai, an Israeli software designer who often found himself frustrated by traffic on his daily commute. In 2013 Shabtai sold the company to Google for a price in excess of $1 billion. While the app is popular in other countries, including the United States, in Israel it has become a phenomenon. Waze representatives say that 90 percent of Israeli drivers have downloaded the app. For Israelis the Waze slogan says it all: "Outsmarting traffic. Together."

Quoted in Ruth Eglash and William Booth, "Israeli Drivers Forgo Traditional GPS Devices to Ride Waze Craze," *Washington Post*, June 11, 2013. www.washingtonpost.com.

A self-driving car winds through the city of Mountain View, California. Proponents of these smart cars say that they will have numerous benefits, including allowing aging, physically challenged, or visually impaired people to travel safely without having to drive.

only one led to an actual crash. MIT engineers say the three "failures" were mainly caused by communication delays between the ITS vehicle and an outside workstation transmitting data about the other cars. The delays showed that if calculations about position and speed are off by even a fraction of a second, disaster can strike. "So you may end up actually being in the capture set while the vehicles think you are not," says MIT mechanical engineer Domitilla Del Vecchio. Another potential problem is a system that is programmed to be too cautious. In that case, Del Vecchio says, "you get a system that gives you warnings even when you don't feel them as necessary. Then you would say, 'Oh, this warning system doesn't work,' and you would neglect it all the time."[31]

The success rate for avoiding collisions in MIT's computerized vehicles is impressive, but AI-based cars still have more to prove. Says science journalist Clay Dillow:

Of course, all of this has to take place in an instant in the real world, and adding more cars and more variables (pedestrians and cyclists, for instance) compounds the challenges. But the work is important for reasons that go beyond the roadway. If we're truly going to learn to live alongside our robots, we don't just need to know what they are going to do next. To some degree, they need to be able to predict our next moves as well.[32]

Vehicle-to-Vehicle Connectivity

One way to improve how well vehicles operate together on the road is to connect them on a wireless network. This breakthrough is made possible by the so-called Internet of Things—the network of objects, from phones to vehicles to buildings, all connected with electronics and software in order to compile and exchange data. From this technology comes the idea of vehicle-to-vehicle connectivity, or V2V, also called integrated navigation. The market for AI-related connected-car products is already beginning to take off. One wireless industry group predicts that by 2018 spending on V2V devices and accessories for automobiles will rise to more than $50 billion. Soon, when a driver pulls out of the garage, he or she will automatically connect to an entire ecosystem of wirelessly connected vehicles, all working together for a safer and more efficient driving experience.

The federal government and major automakers are working collectively to make V2V a reality. For the past decade the National Highway Traffic Safety Administration (NHTSA) has led research into the technology, along with eight automobile companies: Ford, General Motors, Honda, Hyundai, Mercedes-Benz, Nissan, Toyota, and Volkswagen. For the system to work properly, the government must set standards so that all the companies use compatible technology. In other words, their cars must be able to talk to each other. Apart from this ability to communicate, many of the safety technologies required for V2V are already available, albeit mostly in high-end vehicles. These technologies include laser and radar sensors that monitor surrounding traffic and obstacles and automatic braking systems that kick in should the driver be unable to respond in time to warnings of an emergency. Vehicles in the system will communicate on a dedicated segment of wireless spectrum and will employ a new wireless standard so that each message can be authenticated. The computers aboard a V2V-equipped car will process readings broadcast by surrounding vehicles about ten times a second, adjusting their calculations of a possible crash with each new input. They will also learn a driver's tendencies as to acceleration, braking, and steering and make any necessary allowances for variations. And most of the time all this will proceed silently, with drivers scarcely aware of the complex networking taking place.

From 2012 to 2014 the NHTSA and the University of Michigan conducted tests with three thousand cars equipped with experimental V2V transmitters. A review of the vehicles' message records led NHTSA officials to conclude that V2V technology could prevent half a million accidents and more than a thousand fatalities each year. These tests convinced automakers to speed up their rollout of V2V cars, trucks, and SUVs. "I hear estimates all the time on people rolling it out," says Debra Bezzina, senior project manager at the University of Michigan Transportation Research Institute. "It is very close to being production ready."[33] According to Scott Belcher, president of the Intelligent Transportation Society of America, "We think this is really the future of transportation safety, and it's going to make a huge difference in the way we live our lives."[34]

Dispensing with Drivers and Pilots

As V2V technology advances, it comes closer to another AI-based innovation: driverless vehicles. In December 2015 California police stopped one of Google's prototype driverless cars for driving too slow—only 24 miles per hour (39 kph) in a 35 mile-per-hour (56 kph) zone. Pundits across the country joked about Google's computerized student driver being overly cautious. But the firm later explained that nothing went wrong. Operating the car at slower speeds allows engineers to focus on things they

Insurance for Smart Cars

Artificial intelligence is often labeled a disruptive technology for the large changes it can bring to different industries. One example concerns the auto insurance industry, which is bracing for the advent of self-driving cars. For a business that depends on collisions, AI-equipped vehicles are an alarming development. As automakers roll out cars with the ability to avoid accidents, drivers will require much less insurance coverage, and insurers' revenues are likely to plummet. Industry observers predict that premiums customers pay—a total of $195 billion in 2014—could fall by as much as 60 percent over fifteen years. Billionaire investor Warren Buffett sees major trouble ahead for insurers. "If you could come up with anything involved in driving that cut accidents by 30 percent, 40 percent, 50 percent, that would be wonderful," says Buffett. "But we would not be holding a party at our insurance company."

Meanwhile, insurers are looking at other issues related to AI-equipped vehicles. For example, there is the question of who is liable if a self-driving car causes an accident. Some experts say the auto manufacturer would have to assume responsibility, even if a person was behind the wheel. In fact, insurers see a new opportunity in selling high-priced coverage to automakers that build driverless cars. And then there is the related issue of who is at fault if a human driver disables an AI system and then causes a preventable crash. The brave new world of insuring smart cars promises lots of interesting dilemmas.

Quoted in Noah Buhayar and Peter Robison, "Can the Insurance Industry Survive Driverless Cars?," Bloomberg, July 30, 2015. www.bloomberg.com.

want to study, such as placement of sensors and performance of the self-driving software. Also, they prefer to test the vehicle on safer neighborhood streets. Google officials also noted that the car, like others in its driverless fleet, is programmed to consult its own library of sirens, so that when a police car or emergency vehicle approaches, it will drive even more conservatively until it can find the source of the wailing sound. Special cameras on board can also detect flashing lights, causing the car to stop until the source of the lights has passed. Apparently, the car's brush with the police did not cause the onboard computer to panic. There was no word about the officer's reaction to an empty front seat.

Bicyclists travel alongside automobile traffic in London, England. One of the challenges of developing self-driving smart cars is making sure they are capable of taking into account pedestrians and bicyclists, as well as other vehicles, to avoid accidents.

Google engineers claim their self-driving car project offers several benefits. Such cars would allow aging, physically challenged, or visually impaired people to get around in safety and comfort without having to drive. Commuters could do something else during their drive instead of watching the road. Driverless cars could be used on demand and then left in place for the next customer, reducing the need for parking lots and garages. And by developing their own networking innovations, self-driving cars could work together to eliminate accidents and fatalities.

Google's driverless vehicles use AI technology to constantly process information from maps and sensors. This enables them to pinpoint their location and predict the movements of other objects, including cyclists and pedestrians. The cars automatically choose a safe speed and maintain the proper distance from obstacles or other vehicles. Passengers only have to get inside and push a button to go wherever they wish. Google claims that during the six years of the project—covering some 2 million miles (3.2 million km) of travel—its self-driving cars have been involved in only seventeen accidents, none serious. For example, in an incident on February 14, 2016, a Google car going 2 mph (3.2 kph) sideswiped a bus that was traveling at 15 mph (24.1 kph). Google officials explained that their car expected the bus to yield.

If cars can do without drivers, say some scientists, then airplanes might dispense with pilots. The same advances in computing power, sensor technology, and AI that allow for self-driving cars may also lead to pilotless aircraft. Today the US government, together with aviation industry engineers, is exploring how to replace pilots and copilots with AI-equipped robots or remote sensors. "The industry is starting to come out and say we are willing to put our R&D [research and development] money into that,"[35] says Parimal Kopardekar, head of an autonomous systems project at NASA's Ames Research Center.

Commercial planes already do most of their own navigation. A recent survey of pilots flying Boeing 777s found that on a typical flight, they spend only seven minutes manually operating the aircraft. NASA officials believe that someday a number of pilotless planes in flight could be monitored from a control center on the ground by a single "copilot." According to Mary Cummings, a former air force pilot and current director of the Humans and Autonomy Lab at Duke University, the technology exists today. "Planes can already fly themselves," says Cummings. "You're going to need backup capability where a plane can be landed from the ground, or it lands itself."[36] Once such a system is in place, she predicts, pilotless flights could become a reality, first for cargo jets and then for passenger aircraft. And military data on drone tests show that pilotless flights crash less often than piloted ones.

AI for Air Traffic Control

While AI-equipped aircraft are starting to fly themselves, DARPA believes AI could also help manage crowded airspace above battlefields and war zones of the future. Lockheed Martin's Advanced Technology Laboratories is developing a new software system for military air traffic control called the Generalized Integrated Learning Architecture (GILA). The AI software learns the skills of an air traffic controller by gathering knowledge in various ways, some of which include observing experts, accumulating data, asking pointed what-if questions, and employing its own ability to reason. Lockheed engineers claim that GILA often can learn complicated tasks after studying only one example. Its main job is to manage airspace in chaotic battlefield situations by delivering clear and timely orders much like human controllers. GILA will also help air force officials by maintaining a virtual library of the skills it learns from expert operators who rotate out of the service. "GILA will revolutionize the way expert skill and knowledge are captured and transferred," says Ken Whitebread, chief scientist at Lockheed's Intelligent Robotics Lab. "Using planning, learning and reasoning technologies, GILA will know what to learn, why it's important to learn it, and how to focus resources to quickly achieve that learning."[37]

Whether on the roadways or in the skies, AI technology increasingly is affecting the way people get from one place to another. Computer programs can teach themselves how to make travel safer, cheaper, and more efficient. One day intelligent machines may control almost all means of travel. Only time will tell how human societies make use of this exciting—and also potentially disruptive—possibility.

Chapter 5

An Interconnected World

Tim Ahn is a full-time driver for United Parcel Service (UPS), delivering packages each day along his route in Gettysburg, Pennsylvania. Every morning, as Ahn clocks in on his UPS tablet to begin his shift, he faces a choice of two ways to make his deliveries. He can use the old method that combines union work rules and traditional company procedures to decide the order of his stops. Or he can use UPS's new AI-based computer platform called ORION, for On-Road Integrated Optimization and Navigation. If Ahn chooses the old system, UPS does not object but does require him to explain his decision.

Determining the possible delivery routes Ahn could use to make his average of 120 stops per day is not a simple process. The number of alternatives for arranging those stops—taking into account special delivery times, road closures, traffic conditions, and other factors—is 6,689,502,913,449,135 followed by 183 zeros. Figuring the most efficient possible route, even if such a route exists,

WORDS IN CONTEXT

optimization
Selection of the best option or element from a number of available alternatives.

is far beyond the capacity of a human mind. But ORION's AI algorithm is ready to help. "Can a human really think of the best way to deliver 120 stops?" asks Jack Levis, senior director of process management at UPS. "This is where the algorithm will come in. It will explore paths of doing things you would not, because there are just too many combinations."[38]

A More Practical and Efficient System

ORION is UPS's attempt to solve a classic computational dilemma called the traveling salesman problem. This calls for the shortest

Drivers for UPS, like the one shown here delivering parcels, have the option to use an AI-based system to aid them in deciding on the most efficient order in which to make their deliveries. Computers are generally much more effective at such tasks because they can evaluate a far greater number of options than the human brain can.

distance connecting a series of points scattered on a map. In many ways ORION's approach to this problem is typical of AI technology in today's world. It relies on computing power, the interconnectedness of data sources, and the logical technique based on informed guesswork called heuristics. Its thousand-page algorithm, written by a team of fifty UPS engineers, does not seek the perfect answer to the route problem, just the most practical one based on current experience and available data. ORION constantly works to strike a balance between an optimum route and consistent, practical results. Levis points out that consistency is important to customers and drivers alike. "For example, regular business customers who receive packages on a daily basis don't want UPS to show up at 10 a.m. one day, and 5 p.m. the next," he says. "And a customer who is expecting a shipment of frozen food needs delivery as soon as possible, even if efficiency demands that someone gets priority."[39]

ORION is always learning and filing away solutions in order to make the next route proceed more smoothly. The platform's perpetual tweaks to a driver's daily route are carried out on a network of more than fifty-five thousand routes in the United States alone. Just as stock-trading algorithms can deliver large profits by earning fractions of a cent over and over, ORION's small efficiencies in mileage and fuel usage can result in hefty savings over time. UPS CEO David Abney expects ORION to save the company $300 million to $400 million a year.

Machines with Intuitions and Instincts

UPS's ORION platform incorporates certain core advances of AI that make it such a useful technology. These include data mining, or the ability to comb through vast amounts of data at great speed; machine learning, or the ability to get better at something based on data inputs and analysis of results; and probabilistic modeling, or the ability to weigh uncertainties and recommend practical solutions. According to Jerry Kaplan, a professor at the Center for Legal Informatics at Stanford University:

> **WORDS IN CONTEXT**
>
> **probabilistic modeling**
> The ability to weigh uncertainties and recommend practical solutions.

> To date, there seem to be no limitations on just how expert machine learning programs can become. Current programs appear to grow smarter in proportion to the amount of examples they have access to, and the volume of example data grows every day. Freed from dependence on humans to codify and spoon-feed the needed insight, or to instruct them as to how to solve the problem, today's machine learning systems rapidly exceed the capabilities of their creators, solving problems that no human could reasonably be expected to tackle. . . . They are best understood as developing their own intuitions and acting on

Robots in the Labor Force

More workers than ever are worrying about robots stealing their jobs. Today there are on average sixty-six robots for every ten thousand workers worldwide, says a 2015 report from the investment service company Bank of America Merrill Lynch. That does not sound too alarming. But in a highly automated sector like the Japanese car industry, the number of robots per 10,000 workers rises to 1,520. That number represents a lot of displaced workers, and it indicates the trend in AI-related job losses on a global scale. The robots in Japan's car factories are able to work around the clock without supervision for about thirty days at a time, making them very reliable employees. Some economists estimate that replacing human workers with AI-equipped robots can save 90 percent of labor costs. And the robots never take coffee breaks.

It has generally been thought that only limited types of jobs could be replaced by automation. For most jobs, machines lack the needed dexterity or ability to make decisions. But as AI and related technologies advance, these assumptions become less certain. The US Postal Service once employed humans for all letter sorting but now mostly use machines able to recognize human handwriting. Interconnected computers can check credit ratings and perform customer service with peak efficiency. "We are in danger, for the first time in history, of creating a large number of people who are not needed," says economist Andrew Simms. "The question should be, what sort of economy do you want, and to meet what human needs?"

Quoted in Heather Stewart, "Robot Revolution: Rise of 'Thinking' Machines Could Exacerbate Inequality," *Guardian* (Manchester), November 4, 2015. www.theguardian.com.

instinct: a far cry from the old canard that they "can only do what they are programmed to do."[40]

So, although AI programs still cannot approach the complex thinking processes of the human mind, they can already perform certain tasks as well as or even better than a person. AI technology also benefits from the explosive growth of the so-called Internet of Things, in which devices worldwide are connected to the web and are able to collect, store, and share mountains of data. According to Gary Schmitt, director of the American Enterprise Institute's Marilyn Ware Center for Security Studies:

If Cisco Systems' [a large information technology firm] analysis is correct, some 75 billion devices—from kitchen ovens to nuclear power plants, from medical implants to satellites in space—will be connected to the Internet by the end of this decade. Through the narrow lens of access, it appears that we're living [in] a digital utopia: Information can be shared instantaneously, with little regard to borders or nationality.[41]

The result will be an AI-based interconnected world, the implications of which are still uncertain.

What is certain is that people will have to learn to adapt to AI technology. This is already occurring with the help of so-called integrative AI, in which computer systems can see, understand, and converse with humans due to natural language processing and machine learning. People today think nothing of asking a smartphone questions, following an onboard computer's driving directions at rush hour, or consulting an app to translate a foreign phrase. "We see more and more of these successes in daily life," notes Eric Horvitz, managing director of Microsoft Research's Redmond Lab. "We quickly grow accustomed to them and come to expect them."[42]

For all the current interest and excitement, most computer scientists maintain that the biggest advances in AI are probably years away, perhaps decades. Horvitz observes that implementing AI has almost always proved more difficult than first expected. However, what began as a trickle of innovation is rapidly becoming, for better or worse, a cascade of change.

AI's Potential for Solving Problems

Futurists, those scientists and philosophers who ponder the effects of technological change, are divided on how AI will influence human society. On the one hand, many of them predict far-reaching benefits. In an open letter signed by more than eighty-five hundred scientists, the Future of Life Institute writes, "The potential benefits [of AI] are huge, since everything that civilization has to offer is a product of human intelligence; we cannot predict what we might achieve when this intelligence is magnified by the tools AI may provide, but the eradication of disease and poverty are not unfathomable."[43]

Examples in health care are already on the horizon. Robots with AI capability could help care for an aging population. Microscopic AI-based sensors inside a person's body could constantly check for potential problems, such as early warning signs of cancer or heart disease. Global computer networks are already assisting doctors in identifying and dealing with deadly viruses that threaten to become epidemic, such as Ebola or avian flu. For example, AI programs enable scientists to look at thousands of flu strains from around the world simultaneously. Machine-learning algorithms analyze the virus genomes, or genetic makeup, helping scientists determine the mechanisms that transform a pig or bird virus into one that infects humans and for which people have

The "things" in the so-called Internet of Things—in which many types of devices are connected to the Internet—range from kitchen ovens to space satellites (pictured). According to projections, 75 billion items will be connected in this way by the year 2020.

no natural defenses. AI-equipped supercomputers could also analyze the genetic basis of other diseases and aid in the development of new treatments. The resulting improvements in the population's overall health stand to save astronomical sums in health care costs, not to mention the reduction in human misery over time.

In the realm of industry, AI is being used today on a massive scale to manage companies' inventories and deliveries. Some scientists believe interconnected AI-based systems could one day help solve problems of food production and distribution worldwide. If food, energy, and natural resources could be shared globally in an equitable way, poverty could be greatly reduced, they say, and potential sources of conflict would disappear. Machines powered by AI could increasingly do dangerous, dirty, or boring work that humans prefer not to do, enabling people to focus more on interesting tasks or leisure activities. There are also futurists who insist that advances in AI and machine learning are necessary to address the world's most vexing problems, such as climate change and geopolitical conflicts. Researchers at the Human Computation Institute and Cornell University in Ithaca, New York, believe that these so-called wicked problems are so complex that AI must be combined with crowdsourcing (making use of knowledge and data from large groups of people) to offer possible solutions.

> **WORDS IN CONTEXT**
>
> **crowdsourcing**
> Making use of knowledge and data from large groups of people.

Potential Pitfalls of Artificial Intelligence

Other futurists are more fearful about AI's potential. Some worry that AI-based automation—with machines able to do things faster and cheaper than humans—will eliminate jobs on a massive scale and cause huge disruptions to the world economy. The world's wealth could fall to the control of those who own the machines, leaving members of a vast underclass to fend for themselves. One high-profile figure who has expressed concern about the economics of AI is British physicist Stephen Hawking. He says:

If machines produce everything we need, the outcome will depend on how things are distributed. Everyone can enjoy a life of luxurious leisure if the machine-produced wealth is shared, or most people can end up miserably poor if the machine-owners successfully lobby against wealth redistribution. So far, the trend seems to be toward the second option, with technology driving ever-increasing inequality.[44]

Some AI researchers see the interconnectedness associated with AI systems as a major problem. As with the 2010 AI-driven Flash Crash on Wall Street, interconnected computer systems could cause widespread damage in a matter of seconds. Science writer George Dvorsky says such an AI-related disaster would probably be containable by humans, but just barely. "It'll likely arise from an expert system or super-sophisticated algorithm run amok," he says. "And the worry is not so much its power—which is definitely a significant part of the equation—but the speed at which it will inflict the damage. By the time we have a grasp on what's going on, something terrible may have happened."[45] As more AI systems are linked, infrastructure becomes increasingly computer based and interconnected and therefore more vulnerable. An AI program could mistakenly knock out the electric grid, cause a meltdown at a nuclear power plant, or unleash a deadly virus—either biological or digital. Unless reliable safeguards are built in, the odds for this kind of catastrophe are disturbingly high.

The military push for so-called smart weapons also invites trouble, say some futurists. There are already drones that can be programmed to knock out targets halfway around the world. Scientists worry that AI technology will soon create a sort of third revolution in warfare, after gunpowder and nuclear arms. Should a major military power acquire AI-based weapons, a global arms race to match the capability would almost certainly follow.

Military experts say the idea of autonomous killer robots rampaging on the battlefield is pure fiction at this point. Nonetheless, steps are being taken to ensure that weapons remain under human control. In 2012 the US Department of Defense banned the development of autonomous and semiautonomous weapons for ten years. Discussing the issue of AI for military use, Patrick Lin, a

This illustration depicts a futuristic soldier at war. Although fully automated robot soldiers are far from being a reality, some experts do fear that AI could be used to create such weapons or other machines that might one day pose a threat to humans.

professor of philosophy at California Polytechnic State University, says, "We're pushing new frontiers in artificial intelligence. And a lot of people are rightly skeptical that it would ever advance to the point where it has anything called full autonomy." But as Lin admits, "No one is really an expert on predicting the future."[46]

Certain scientists see nothing but dire consequences from artificial intelligence. Hawking is on record that AI, however useful it is for now, could one day pose a threat to the human race. "It would take off on its own, and re-design itself at an ever increasing rate," he says. "Humans, who are limited by slow biological evolution, couldn't compete, and would be superseded."[47]

AI and the Singularity

Hawking's unease about AI is reserved for some date far in the future. Computer scientists believe that at some point, machines could develop a superhuman intelligence, including the ability to reason and improve themselves endlessly. This ultimate change is known as strong AI. For now, humanity is experiencing the rise of weak AI—expert systems that equal or surpass human intelligence only in narrowly defined activities, not in an overall sense. This form of AI is certainly not weak, however. It can direct rush hour traffic, sort and analyze millions of genetic mutations, regulate power plants, and perform thousands of other enormously complex tasks. Many scientists are leery of the lack of safeguards with weak AI, fearing these systems could lurch out of control at a moment's notice. But the potential rewards and disasters associated with weak AI are nothing compared to what might be in store for humanity should strong AI emerge.

Futurists associate the development of strong AI—vastly superior machine intelligence—with something called the Singularity. This is the point at which technological change becomes so extreme that human life is fundamentally altered forever. Such a change would have an explosive impact on every aspect of life. It would be what mathematician Irving John Good described in 1965 as an intelligence explosion:

> Let an ultra-intelligent machine be defined as a machine that can far surpass all the intellectual activities of any man however clever. Since the design of machines is one of these intellectual activities, an ultra-intelligent machine could design even better machines; there would then unquestionably be an "intelligence explosion," and the intelligence of man would be left far behind.[48]

The idea of the Singularity was popularized by Vernor Vinge, a science fiction writer, in a 1993 essay, "Technological Singularity."

Vinge described it as "a point where our old models must be discarded and a new reality rules. As we move closer to this point, it will loom vaster and vaster over human affairs."[49] More recently, the American inventor and futurist Ray Kurzweil has forecast the year 2045 as the likely arrival date of the Singularity. He believes the event will include aspects of AI, robotics, molecular biology, genetics, and nanotechnology (the science of microscopic things). Superintelligent computers, says Kurzweil, will enable scientists to unlock the genetic secrets of aging and extend the human life span. People might one day merge with machines, downloading their memories and personalities into mechanical shells to

Kurzweil on the Singularity

Ray Kurzweil is a scientist and inventor. He is passionately interested in the possibilities for the Singularity, an AI-driven future of massive technological change. The following is excerpted from an interview with John Brockman:

> The kind of scenarios I'm talking about 20 or 30 years from now are not being developed because there's one laboratory that's sitting there creating a human-level intelligence in a machine. They're happening because it's the inevitable end result of thousands of little steps. . . . If you take thousands of those little steps—which are getting faster and faster—you end up with some remarkable changes. . . .
>
> [The Singularity is] a merger between human intelligence and machine intelligence that is going to create something bigger than itself. It's the cutting edge of evolution on our planet. One can make a strong case that it's actually the cutting edge of the evolution of intelligence in general, because there's no indication that it's occurred anywhere else. To me that is what human civilization is all about. It is part of our destiny and part of the destiny of evolution to continue to progress ever faster, and to grow the power of intelligence exponentially. . . . What human beings are is a species that has undergone a cultural and technological evolution, and it's the nature of evolution that it accelerates, and that its powers grow exponentially, and that's what we're talking about.

Quoted in John Brockman, "The Singularity: A Talk with Ray Kurzweil," *Edge*, March 24, 2001. https://edge.org.

form cyborgs with amazing capabilities. Kurzweil's version of the Singularity promises unlimited intelligence, wealth, freedom, and leisure for the human race. Other futurists think it is just as likely to bring global catastrophe from swarms of intelligent robots, perhaps too small to be seen with the naked eye. Or they predict that AI systems will ultimately enslave the human race or make it irrelevant. As Bill Joy, the cofounder of Sun Microsystems, has phrased it, "The future doesn't need us."[50]

Whether or not the Singularity ever arrives, breakthroughs in AI technology will continue to increase the interconnectedness of the world. New generations will probably take AI for granted and learn to use it in unforeseen ways. Artificial intelligence could ultimately be viewed not as a threat but as a valuable tool.

Source Notes

Introduction: Fast Track for a Supercomputer

1. Bob Pisani, "Three Years After "Jeopardy,' IBM Gets Serious About Watson," CNBC, October 8, 2014. www.cnbc.com.
2. Jurica Dujmovic, "Opinion: Artificial Intelligence Is Creeping into Our Everyday Lives," MarketWatch, September 12, 2014. www.marketwatch.com.
3. Quoted in Guia Marie Del Prado, "18 Artificial Intelligence Researchers Reveal the Profound Changes Coming to Our Lives," Tech Insider, October 26, 2015. www.techinsider.io.

Chapter 1: Making Machines That Can Think

4. Quoted in Amina Khan, "Humans Take Note: Artificial Intelligence Just Got a Lot Smarter," *Los Angeles Times*, December 10, 2015. http://touch.latimes.com.
5. A.M. Turing, "Computing Machinery and Intelligence," *Mind*, 1950. www.loebner.net.
6. Quoted in Keith Vander Linden, "Notes on Intelligent Machines," Department of Computer Science, Calvin College, 2001. http://cs.calvin.edu.
7. Quoted in BBC, "AI: 15 Key Moments in the Story of Artificial Intelligence," 2016. www.bbc.co.uk.
8. Bruce G. Buchanan, "A (Very) Brief History of Artificial Intelligence," *AI Magazine*, Winter 2005. www.aaai.org.
9. Quoted in Gina Kolata, "Computer Math Proof Shows Reasoning Power," *New York Times*, December 10, 1996. www.nytimes.com.
10. Jerry Kaplan, *Humans Need Not Apply: A Guide to Wealth and Work in the Age of Artificial Intelligence*. New Haven: Yale University Press, 2015, p. 24.
11. Quoted in Stephen F. DeAngelis, "The Upside of Artificial Intelligence Development," *Wired*. www.wired.com.

Chapter 2: Speeding into Business and Marketing

12. Quoted in Jim Zarroli, "Who, or What, Crashed the Market in a Flash in 2010?," NPR, April 27, 2015. www.npr.org.
13. Quoted in Georgia McCafferty, "Artificial Intelligence Is the Next Big Thing for Hedge Funds Seeking an Edge," *Quartz*, May 4, 2015. http://qz.com.
14. Quoted in Adrian Wan, "Hong Kong Start-Up to Bet Millions on Hedge Fund Run by Artificial Intelligence," *South China Morning Post* (Hong Kong), April 24, 2015. www.scmp.com.
15. Quoted in Arjun Kharpal, "How AI Could Make You a Top Stock-Picker," CNBC, July 9, 2015. www.cnbc.com.
16. Quoted in Karen Boman, "Cognitive Worker Amelia Could Transform Oil, Gas Operations," Rigzone, August 7, 2015. www.rigzone.com.
17. Quoted in Jason Ankeny, "Meet Amelia, the AI Platform That Could Change the Future of IT," *Entrepreneur*, May 26, 2015. www.entrepreneur.com.
18. Quoted in Nick Heath, "Why AI Could Destroy More Jobs than It Creates, and How to Save Them," *TechRepublic*, August 19, 2014. www.techrepublic.com.
19. Quoted in Jack Clark, "Google Turning Its Lucrative Web Search Over to AI Machines," Bloomberg, October 26, 2015. www.bloomberg.com.
20. Quoted in Marty Swant, "6 Ways Google's Artificial Intelligence Could Impact Search Engine Marketing," *Adweek*, November 2, 2015. www.adweek.com.
21. Quoted in Alex Iskold, "Q&A with Mona—A.I. Based Personal Shopping Assistant," *Alex Iskold* (blog), December 13, 2015. http://alexiskold.net.

Chapter 3: Doctors in a Box

22. Quoted in Daniela Hernandez, "Artificial Intelligence Is Now Telling Doctors How to Treat You," *Wired*, June 2, 2014. www.wired.org.
23. Quoted in Hernandez, "Artificial Intelligence Is Now Telling Doctors How to Treat You."

24. Robert S. Ledley and Lee B. Lusted, "Reasoning Foundations of Medical Diagnosis," *Science*, July 3, 1959. www.cs.tufts.edu.
25. Christopher de la Torre, "The AI Doctor Is Ready to See You," Singularity Hub, May 10, 2010. http://singularityhub.com.
26. Quoted in Barbara Boughton, "Teachable Software May Help Diagnose Endocarditis, Study Shows," Medscape, September 18, 2009. www.medscape.com.
27. Quoted in Adam Conner-Simons, "How a Computer Can Help Your Doctor Better Diagnose Cancer," *MIT News*, April 23, 2015. http://news.mit.edu.
28. Mike Orcutt, "Why IBM Just Bought Billions of Medical Images for Watson to Look At," *MIT Technology Review*, August 11, 2015. www.technologyreview.com.
29. Quoted in Jessica Leber, "IBM's Watson Tackles the Tumor Genome, on the Way to Personalized Cancer Treatments," *Co.Exist*, March 19, 2014. www.fastcoexist.com.

Chapter 4: Smarter and Safer Travel

30. Quoted in Bradley Berman, "How AI Turns Traffic Lights into Intelligent Agents," *ReadWrite* (blog), January 22, 2014. http://readwrite.com.
31. Quoted in Emily Finn, "'Smart Cars' That Are Actually, Well, Smart," *MIT News*, June 14, 2011. http://news.mit.edu.
32. Clay Dillow, "MIT Demonstrates Smart Cars That Predict Each Others' Moves to Avoid Collisions," *Popular Science*, June 14, 2011. www.popsci.com.
33. Quoted in Olivia Marcus, "Car-to-Car Communication May Hit Roads Soon," *U.S. News & World Report*, March 4, 2015. www.usnews.com.
34. Quoted in Stephen F. DeAngelis, "Business and Artificial Intelligence," *Enterra Solutions* (blog), March 12, 2013. www.enterrasolutions.com.
35. Quoted in John Markoff, "Planes Without Pilots," *New York Times*, April 6, 2015. www.nytimes.com.
36. Quoted in Chris Isidore, "Would Pilotless Planes Make Sense?," CNNMoney, March 27, 2015. http://money.cnn.com.

37. Quoted in Lewis Page, "DARPA Continues Military AI Air-Traffic Project," *Register* (London), February 12, 2008. www.theregister.co.uk.

Chapter 5: An Interconnected World

38. Quoted in Steven Rosenbush and Laura Stevens, "At UPS, the Algorithm Is the Driver," *Wall Street Journal*, February 16, 2015. www.wsj.com.
39. Quoted in Rosenbush and Stevens, "At UPS, the Algorithm Is the Driver."
40. Kaplan, *Humans Need Not Apply*, p. 30.
41. Gary Schmitt, "Waging War in Zeros and Ones," *Wall Street Journal*, February 25, 2016. www.wsj.com.
42. Quoted in Phys.org, "The Future of Artificial Intelligence," July 7, 2015. http://phys.org.
43. Future of Life Institute, "An Open Letter: Research Priorities for Robust and Beneficial Artificial Intelligence." http://futureoflife.org.
44. Quoted in *New Reddit Journal of Science*, "Science AMA Series: Stephen Hawking AMA Answers," October 8, 2015. www.reddit.com.
45. George Dvorsky, "How Much Longer Before Our First AI Catastrophe?," *Gizmodo* (blog), April 1, 2013. http://io9.gizmodo.com.
46. Quoted in Will Knight, "Military Robots: Armed, but How Dangerous?," *MIT Technology Review*, August 3, 2015. www.technologyreview.com.
47. Quoted in Michael Casey, "Stephen Hawking Warns Artificial Intelligence Could Be Threat to Human Race," CBS News, December 3, 2014. www.cbsnews.com.
48. Irving John Good, "Speculations Concerning the First Ultra-intelligent Machine," Wayback Machine. https://web.archive.org.
49. Quoted in Annalee Newlitz, "What Is the Singularity and Will You Live to See It?," *Gizmodo* (blog), May 10, 2010. http://io9.gizmodo.com.
50. Quoted in "Top 10 Reasons We Should Fear the Singularity," *Singularity Weblog*, May 22, 2012. www.singularityweblog.com.

For Further Research

Books

James Barrat, *Our Final Invention: Artificial Intelligence and the End of the Human Era*. New York: St. Martin's, 2015.

Pedro Domingos, *The Master Algorithm: How the Quest for the Ultimate Learning Machine Will Remake Our World*. New York: Basic Books, 2015.

Jerry Kaplan, *Humans Need Not Apply: A Guide to Wealth and Work in the Age of Artificial Intelligence*. New York: Yale University Press, 2015.

Ray Kurzweil, *The Singularity Is Near: When Humans Transcend Biology*. New York: Penguin, 2006.

Robert Wachter, *The Digital Doctor: Hope, Hype, and Harm at the Dawn of Medicine's Computer Age*. New York: McGraw-Hill Education, 2015.

Internet Sources

Jack Clark, "Google Turning Its Lucrative Web Search Over to AI Machines," Bloomberg, October 26, 2015. www.bloomberg .com/news/articles/2015-10-26/google-turning-its-lucrative-web -search-over-to-ai-machines.

Nick Heath, "Why AI Could Destroy More Jobs than It Creates, and How to Save Them," *TechRepublic*, August 19, 2014. www .techrepublic.com/article/ai-is-destroying-more-jobs-than-it-cre ates-what-it-means-and-how-we-can-stop-it.

Daniela Hernandez, "Artificial Intelligence Is Now Telling Doc-tors How to Treat You," *Wired*, June 2, 2014. www.wired.com /2014/06/ai-healthcare.

Robert McMillan, "AI Has Arrived, and That Really Worries the World's Brightest Minds," *Wired*, January 16, 2015. www.wired .com/2015/01/ai-arrived-really-worries-worlds-brightest-minds.

Mike Orcutt, "Why IBM Just Bought Billions of Medical Images for Watson to Look At," *MIT Technology Review*, August 11, 2015. www.technologyreview.com/s/540141/why-ibm-just-bought-bill ions-of-medical-images-for-watson-to-look-at.

Websites

Association for the Advancement of Artificial Intelligence (www.aaai.org). This nonprofit scientific society promotes research into AI and public understanding of its future possibilities. The association's website includes a news page devoted to the latest topics in AI research.

Computer History Museum (www.computerhistory.org). This website presents an entertaining and informative timeline of the development of computers and AI technology. It features period photographs and colorful graphics, as well as information about topics related to AI, such as robotics, networking, and computer games.

Google Quantum A.I. Lab Team (https://plus.google.com/+ QuantumAILab/posts). Google engineers working on AI post articles, videos, and panel discussions about the latest research in the field.

Turing Test (www.psych.utoronto.ca/users/reingold/courses/ai /turing.html). This website presents a discussion of Alan Turing's famous test for machine intelligence. It also includes sample natural language processing sites where users can test the latest AI capabilities themselves.

Index

Picture Credits

About the Author

John Allen is a writer living in Oklahoma City.